VISION BOARD SUCCESS

HOW TO ACHIEVE ALL
YOUR DREAMS IN LIFE

Christopher Mitchell

www.ChangeYourLifeOvernight.com

VISION BOARD SUCCESS! HOW TO ACHIEVE
ALL YOUR DREAMS IN LIFE!

Copyright © 2017 Christopher Mitchell

ISBN-13: 978-1547035595

ISBN-10: 1547035595

Printed In The United States Of America.

TABLE OF CONTENTS:

The book you're about to read is proof that a vision board works for helping a person achieve their goals and dreams in life. The author shares some real events from his personal life that resulted from having a vision board. He encourages you to think big, post pictures of what you want to achieve in life on a vision board, and believe that all your dreams will come true. If you would like to speak to Christopher, or perhaps join his team and have him become your personal mentor, feel free to contact him at his website. God bless you!

www.ChangeYourLifeOvernight.com

Chapter One:

My Beginning.

In case this is the first book of mine that you've purchased and you have no idea who I am, let me briefly fill you in. My name is Christopher Paul Mitchell. I was born on January 9th, 1979, in Houston, Texas. Two years later, my younger brother was born. Like a lot of couples, my parents were complete opposites. My mom was an angel sent from Heaven, while my dad was the opposite.

When I was three years old my dad cheated on my mom. My mom then divorced my dad and became a single mother. She worked as a secretary at Ohio Wesleyan University in Delaware, Ohio. With a tiny salary to take care of all the monthly bills, she struggled financially to say the least.

Like most single mothers, my mom was constantly stressed from never having enough money. She would drop us off at school in the morning before driving herself to work. My brother and I would walk to the baby sitters house after school and stay there until 7:00 at night when my mom would pick us up. She would then take us home and make us dinner, have us take our baths, get our clothes ready for the next day, and then pray her blessings over us as she tucked us in for the night.

That was the life we lived Monday through Friday. On Saturday and Sunday, the three of us would drive to the ballpark and she would watch us play baseball all weekend long. We loved playing baseball and we loved having mom watch us play. She was the best. She was our hero.

We always wanted to make her proud. She was loving, caring, hard-working, and had the mindset of an entrepreneur. Late at night after she would put us to sleep she would go into the kitchen and bake cookies for several hours. She made the best chocolate chip cookies in the world. To this day, my favorite cheat meal is cookies, all because of my mom. She would bake dozens and dozens of cookies, take them to work with her the next day, and then sell them to her coworkers for some extra money.

She hardly ever slept. She was wonder woman. She was our loving mother. She was our best friend. She was our chauffeur. She was an entrepreneur with a business on the side of her job. And, she made the best cookies in the world. My brother and I loved her more than anything. She was everything to us.

My mom was that person that everyone loved and adored. She would have done anything for anyone. My mom proved her love for others by her actions, not her words. She was a great role model for me and my brother. When I was seven years old, I was sitting on the living room floor with my mom sitting behind me on the couch. I looked at her and said these exact words that I will NEVER forget for as long as I live:

Mom, I'm going to become rich someday, and when I do, I'm going to take care of you and you're never going to struggle again. She looked me in the eyes, told me she believed me, and then started crying. Just two years later when I was nine years old, my mom suddenly died from cancer. It took everyone by surprise. She was only thirty-five years old when she passed away.

My dad automatically regained custody of me and my brother when my mom died. He had remarried and his wife had a daughter of her own. My dad also had a collection of cats and dogs that he couldn't properly care for. My brother and I were now living with my dad, his wife, her daughter, and a total of three cats and ten dogs. It was miserable.

My dad and his wife fought every single day without exception. My dad screamed every single time he opened his mouth. He was a terrible dad and a terrible husband. My brother and I stayed out of the house as much as we could because we feared being around our dad more than we feared the devil. He was very hateful and abusive. My mom was loving and encouraging, while my dad was hateful and abusive. Like I said, they were complete opposites.

My dad and his wife would work at their jobs during the day, then come home at night and do nothing but eat and watch television. Every time they ate something they would use a different dish to eat on. When they were finished eating they would put the dirty dishes in the sink. When the sink filled up they would put the dirty dishes on the counter. After all the counter space was covered they would then pile the dirty dishes on the kitchen table. The entire house was covered with dirty dishes.

They left dirty cups out still filled with soda. They left pizza boxes laying open with the crust still inside. Bugs would be crawling around the house on many different occasions. The bathtub drain was so clogged that every single time you took a shower you would be standing in dirty bath water up to your knees.

I was born with a very outspoken attitude and I don't put up with things that I don't deserve. So, when my dad would yell across the house at me telling me to do the dishes, I would yell back no! I told him he was the one who dirtied all the dishes so he should be the one who cleans them. My dad would start yelling at the top of his lungs, then pick me up and throw me across the room. That was the relationship I had with him.

When I became a freshman in high school I joined the wrestling team and started working out. One day after I arrived home from wrestling practice my dad was in one of his usual rages. He started yelling at me to clean the house and I simply said no. Like always, he didn't like that, so he came toward me to abuse me yet again, but this time something was different. I completely snapped!

I had taken enough abuse from this man. I had gained a lot of size and strength from working out and I refused to get beat again. I defended myself against my dad for the first time. Instead of him throwing me across the room, this time I picked him up and threw him across the room. After I threw him across the room, I ran over to him, put him in a wrestling move and completely popped both of his shoulders out of their sockets. He was in a lot of pain.

His third wife at the time called 911 and the ambulance rushed him to the emergency room. He stayed in the hospital for a few days because of the damage I had done to him physically. When he and his wife came home from the hospital he kicked me out of the house at that very moment. I became homeless at fifteen years old.

I made some phone calls and ended up moving in with a few relatives. I moved in with my grandparents for a while, then I moved in with an Aunt for a while, and then I moved in with an Uncle for a while. I started bouncing around between these relatives houses until I became an official adult. When I turned eighteen years old I received a government check from my mom's death. That check allowed me to buy my first car and move into my own apartment.

I still had five months until I graduated high school, but I was already living in my own apartment. At this point in my life I became a complete loner. I didn't hang out with people anymore. I was now eating healthy and working out every day, while all my so-called high school friends either drank beer or smoked pot. I wasn't about to join them.

All I did was go to school, workout, and go to baseball practice. I hated school, but I had to attend in order to play baseball. Baseball was my life! I was good. Really good! My dream was to become a Major League Baseball Player. I had just one problem. I was small. Really small! That's why I started working out in the first place. I wanted to get bigger, faster, and stronger for baseball.

I went on to graduate high school just like everyone else, despite bouncing around for three years. I received a free college scholarship from Ohio Wesleyan University in honor of my mom. However, I knew college would never teach me how to become rich, so I told them to keep it. I passed on going to college and tried out for the big leagues instead. I went down to Lakeland, Florida to The Detroit Tigers spring training camp.

I was hoping my Major League Baseball career was about to get started, but I started having all kinds of pain in my joints. To make a long story short, I ended up having five surgeries in the next sixteen months on both of my elbows, both of my shoulders, and my right knee. I never played baseball again.

I had no idea what I was going to do with my life now because the only thing I ever dreamed about was playing Major League Baseball. There was no way I was going to get a job and work for the next fifty years just so I could retire dead broke and end up working at Wal-Mart as a greeter until the day I die. I refused to do what the rest of the world did. I knew that 98% of the world's population was miserable in life and I promised myself that would never be me.

To become successful in life, find out what everyone else in the world is doing and do the exact opposite.

That was a quote that I saw on a coffee mug when I was about ten years old and I have never forgot it. I started living by these words from that very moment. So, when I found out that the masses go to college, I decided not to. When I found out that the masses get a job, I decided to be an entrepreneur. When I found out that the masses drink alcohol and smoke cigarettes, I decided to eat organic foods and drink protein smoothies. When I found out that the masses are dead broke, I decided to be rich. I made up my mind at a very early age that whatever I saw the majority of the people in the world doing, I would do the exact opposite. Sure enough, that is exactly what I've done for thirty years now.

I had no idea that coffee mug would teach me such priceless wisdom at such a young age. I've been sharing these same words with people most of my life. Most people get married and then divorce. Most people live paycheck to paycheck their entire lives. Most people eat crappy fast food. Most people accept illness, sickness, and disease. So, I do the exact opposite. I encourage you to do the same. This is probably the best advice that I've ever received, and probably the best advice that I can share with you as well. If you're sick and tired of being sick and tired, or if you're fed up with the life you're currently living, then I encourage you to never forget these amazing words:

To become successful in life, find out what everyone else in the world is doing and do the exact opposite.

Chapter Two:

Association.

Before we begin exploring what a vision board is, I feel like I need to first educate you about the power of association. This is important because if you're associating with the wrong people, which most people do, then a vision board isn't going to do you any good. One of the biggest reasons why 98% of the population is dead broke is because of the poverty-stricken individuals they associate themselves with. The famous quote: *Birds of a feather flock together* is very true.

Since 98% is practically everyone in the world, then there's a very good chance that you're in that group. What I'm going to share with you in this book can help you cross over to the 2% class of the wealthy.

However, in order to do this, you must make some changes. Achieving the lifestyle of your dreams: dream cars and homes, your soulmate, living a long life with perfect health, getting rich, traveling the world, and making a difference in people's lives isn't going to happen by accident. You must create the lifestyle you want to live. The few people who do this do it with passion and purpose.

There are laws that govern how this world operates. The rich use these laws knowingly to their advantage, while the poor use these laws unknowingly to their disadvantage. The laws don't care if you understand them or not. It's your responsibility to learn them so you can start living the life of your dreams. In case you're confused, let me explain some of these laws to you so that you can understand them.

Let me use the Law Of Gravity to start with. The Law Of Gravity states that if something falls it's going to hit the ground every single time. There are no exceptions. I'll prove it to you. It doesn't matter whether a person is young or old, white or black, male or female, smart or ignorant, if they jump off the top of a skyscraper they're going to fall to the ground and die. This is a fact. Not one single person in the entire world can jump off the top of a skyscraper and float upwards. They will always, 100% of the time fall to the ground.

The Law Of Gravity doesn't feel sorry for people if they jump off the top of a skyscraper because they're depressed. Whether the person is in America, Canada, China, or Australia, The Law Of Gravity works the same for everyone. All the laws of the universe do. You must know this!

So, now that you know the laws of the universe work the same for everyone, let me explain to you how The Law Of Association works.

The Law Of Association states that whoever you associate with is who you will soon become.

If you associate with people who drink alcohol every day, then you're going to drink alcohol every day too. If you associate with people who are poor financially, then you're going to be poor financially too. If you associate with people who are fat and unhealthy, then you're going to be fat and unhealthy too. However, if you associate with four different millionaires every single day, then guess what's going to happen? You're going to become the fifth millionaire. Like all laws, The Law Of Association works for everyone.

Whoever you associate with is going to rub off on you. They're going to leave an impression on you and you're going to want to impress them back so they'll accept you into their circle. You'll follow them and do what they do so you can fit in. This is peer pressure and it's more prevalent with adults than it is with children. This is why freshman in high school begin smoking cigarettes. They want to fit in with the upper classmen. However, if you would have asked them when they were in the eighth grade if they want to smoke cigarettes they would have told you absolutely not. This is what the power of association does.

People who once thought clearly and had a sound mind begin to commit crimes because the people who they associate with commit crimes. The Law Of Association is one of the most powerful laws in the entire universe.

This is why it's extremely important to associate with rich and successful people. When you associate with people who have a lot of money you'll learn why. You'll find out that they speak and think differently about money than poor people do. This is why they're rich. As you have a conversation with them you'll notice how they speak about money. Rich and poor people don't associate with each other because they're not compatible. They don't have anything to talk about. Remember the famous quote that I shared a few pages ago: *Birds of a feather flock together?*

Well, now you know what this means. You'll never see chickens associating with eagles. They're not compatible. They don't have anything in common. Chickens are like poor people. They just peck on the ground all day long. They're very depressing to be around.

However, eagles are like rich people. They're very rare. They don't ever peck on the ground. They don't even fly. They soar! They can climb to higher altitudes than airplanes. They like to be above their prey. They like to be on top of the world. They have laser beam focus and can see their target from a mile away. They set their eyes on what they want and go after it with pin point accuracy.

Poor people gave up on all their goals and dreams in life. Every word that comes out of the mouth of a poor person is negative. Get rich? Are you kidding me? They never even think about getting rich. They don't even think that's possible. Working at a job that they hate, sitting in rush hour traffic for two hours every day, and getting that tiny paycheck every two weeks is just fine with them. They only care about themselves.

However, rich people have huge goals and dreams. They're highly focused. They set goals and do whatever it takes to achieve them. You'll never see them slacking off or hear them complain. They let their actions do the talking for them. While poor people are easily distracted, rich people know exactly what they want. When you associate with rich people their habits and mindsets will help you grow and develop into a leader.

If you want to become rich you must associate with rich people. That's all there is to it. Associating with people who have a lot of money will increase your thinking and skyrocket your income. We become like the people we associate with. Winners always associate with other winners. The reason why only a few people ever become millionaires and billionaires is because of their associations.

Rich people speak and think differently about money than poor people do. That's why you need to listen closely to the people you associate with. The words they speak will tell you who they are. Let me give you a few examples of how rich and poor people talk about money so you can recognize the difference.

Poor people say, I hate my job!

Rich people say, I love my business!

Poor people say, I just got a forty cent raise at my job.

Rich people say, I just increased my net worth by twenty million dollars.

Poor people say, I really need a vacation.

Rich people say, I should end this vacation and get back to work.

Poor people say, I can't wait to get paid on Friday so I can buy a new big screen television.

Rich people say, I can't wait to sell my company so I can use the cash to invest in a bigger one.

Poor people say, I'm going to drive the family to the lake this weekend.

Rich people say, I'm going to fly the family to Tahiti this weekend.

Obviously, you can clearly see the difference. These are the types of words you need to listen for. The words that come out of a person's mouth will tell you if that person is rich or poor. If you want to get rich you must associate with rich people as much as possible. Poor people want to meet a millionaire so they can tell their friends they met a millionaire. However, millionaires want to associate with billionaires so they can learn how they think. Poor people are in the stands watching the game. Rich people are on the field playing the game. Which one are you? Are you watching or playing?

You need to write down the top five people in your life that you associate with the most. Take their incomes, add them together, then divide that number by five. The number that appears will be so close to the income you make it will scare you. That's why you must associate with rich people. If you spend all your time with four different millionaires, then guess what? Pretty soon, you'll be the fifth millionaire. This is how The Law Of Association works.

Everyone knows this is true. Big, strong bodybuilders associate with other big, strong bodybuilders.

Religious people associate with other religious people. And of course, rich people associate with other rich people. Again, birds of a feather flock together. So, start associating with rich people and you'll become rich. Rich people are always looking for individuals who are optimistic, goal-oriented, enthusiastic, and who have a positive mental outlook on life. However, rich people do everything in their power to avoid people who are toxic and negative. So, if you're constantly negative and complaining about how crappy life is, you better change immediately. Rich people despise negative people. My life growing up was crappy. It mentally programmed me to live a life of poverty and failure, which I did, until I changed my associations. When I started associating with rich and positive people, I then became one.

Chapter Three:

Vision Board.

If you're new to setting goals then you might not even know what a vision board is. If that happens to be the case for you, let me educate you on this for a minute. A vision board is a plain poster board that you can get at any store that carries basic school supplies. Once you have yourself a plain poster board you then cut out pictures of things you want to be, do, or have in your life and tape them to the board. Look at this vision board every single day and visualize the pictures you put on it. By looking at these pictures every single day you're allowing your imagination to accept them as part of your life right now. Not in the future, but right now! You accept the dream car, the dream house, the dream physical body, the dream vacation spots, the dream spouse, the millions of dollars in your bank account, the charities you want to support, and anything else your imagination can dream of.

By taping pictures of everything you dream of you impregnate your subconscious mind with them repeatedly every single day. The more you look at your vision board the more real this dream lifestyle will become for you. Once you accept this dream lifestyle in your subconscious mind and truly believe that it's possible, new ideas, things, events, and people will start appearing in your life to help you bring it into reality. Very few people in the world have a vision board and very few people in the world are living the life of their dreams. As kids get older they stop dreaming. Once you stop dreaming your life is over.

Every single person that I've ever known who has a vision board has achieved most, if not all the things they were dreaming of. On the flip side however, all the people that I know who don't have a vision board are fat, broke, work at a job that they hate, and are miserable in life. This isn't a mere coincidence. My favorite book in the world is the Holy Bible. In the New Testament Jesus says this:

He called a little child to him, and placed the child among them. And he said: Truly I tell you, unless you change and become like little children, you will never enter the kingdom of heaven. Matthew 18:2-3

Jesus is speaking to adults here. He's telling them to be like little children because little children are innocent. They have great faith. They believe that absolutely anything is possible.

Little children are humble, unlike most adults. Little children believe that God can provide for them, heal them of incurable diseases, and do anything they ask him to. If Jesus is telling us to be like little children, I'm going to listen and do what he says.

Little children have no problem dreaming big dreams. They have no problem seeing themselves driving a Lamborghini. They just let their imaginations run wild. They believe they're going to get whatever they can think of. However, adults don't allow themselves to dream because they filter everything through the amount of money they earn at their dead-end job. They lost their faith as the got older. They lost the power of their imagination. Jesus is telling us not to do this. He's saying, that if you want to enter the kingdom of heaven you MUST be like little children.

Don't ever stop dreaming, and if you have, I encourage you to start dreaming again. A vision board is a very powerful tool that can help you achieve all your dreams in life. If you start looking at pictures of cars, homes, money, vacations, and doing things you love to do every day, your subconscious mind will start believing that it's possible. The more you believe that anything is possible, your faith will begin to grow. Once your faith is fully developed you will then start manifesting things in your life that currently seem impossible.

However, most of the people in the world, 98% to be exact, will tell you that a vision board is bologna, nonsense, and stupid, hocus pocus garbage. Pay them no mind. If they don't drive the car you want, if they don't live in the home you want, if they're not completely debt free with millions of dollars in the bank, if they're not happy in their marriage, if they're not helping the less fortunate, and if they're not absolutely in love with their lifestyle, then don't ever listen to anything they say.

I learned what a vision board was back in 2006, at one of the lowest points in my life. I was very blessed to have a successful businessman named Leonard Trojan introduce me to this way of positive visualization. When I met Mr. Trojan he was driving a hundred thousand dollar Mercedes Benz that was completely paid for, while I was driving a Nissan Sentra with a four hundred dollar a month car payment. He was wearing tailor made suits, where as I was wearing baggy pants and tank tops. All his friends were millionaires, where as all my friends were dead broke. He had perfect communication skills, where as the only thing that came out of my mouth was cuss words. He became my mentor. I listened to everything he told me to do because I wanted the lifestyle that he was living. When he told me to get a vision board, I did so immediately. No questions asked.

I was filled with excitement for the first time in years. I let myself dream again. My imagination was running free like a gazelle out in the wild. I bought all the magazines I could find that had photos of money, sports cars, and expensive homes in them. It was so much fun cutting out photos and taping them to my vision board. I felt like I was a little child back in elementary school doing an art project. I covered my vision board with photos of my dream lifestyle. I was in awe. I stared at that board every moment I could.

I even took a photo and made it my screen saver on my cell phone. Every time I looked at my vision board my faith grew stronger. However, I still had times when I was negative and you will too. The majority of the people in the world are broke and negative. Our environment molds us to their way of thinking. We live in a very negative world. That's why it's very important to not only create a vision board, but to look at it and meditate on it every chance you get.

The more you look at your vision board and hold those pictures in your mind, the faster those things will show up for you in your life. Once I started looking at my vision board every day, some miraculous things started happening for me. Let me share some of the amazing things that have manifested in my life that were once on my vision board.

Chapter Four:

Oprah's Building.

The first time I ever visited Chicago, Illinois, I immediately fell in love with the city. I loved the architecture of all the buildings. I loved the way the river was built through the city and flowed out to Lake Michigan. I loved the big ferris wheel on Navy Pier. I loved all the upscale shopping along Michigan Avenue. I loved all the professional sports teams the city had. But most of all, I loved all the upscale, expensive, luxurious hotels and restaurants.

In the luxurious part of downtown Chicago sits the historic water tower. This area of downtown Chicago is nothing but wealth and opulence. Just walking along the sidewalk on Michigan Avenue made me feel wealthy. Surrounding the water tower sits some of my all-time favorite hotels such as: The Omni, The Peninsula, The Park Hyatt, The Four Seasons, and The Ritz Carlton. All these hotels were built for the rich and successful. Every time my wife and I visit Chicago we stay at one of these hotels. Is it worth it to spend $1,000 per night to stay in one of these hotels? Yes, you better believe it! Is it worth it to spend $200 on brunch at one of these hotels? Yes, you better believe it! Is it worth it to pay $100 per day to valet your rental car at one of these hotels? Yes, you better believe it! This is how the wealthy live and I'm wealthy!

Oh, and if you love fine dining, then you'll absolutely love the exquisite restaurants in Chicago. If you ever visit the windy city here are some of my favorite five star restaurants:

Tru, Alinea, Sixteen, Bandera, North Pond, Del Frisco's, Joe's Seafood, and Benny's Chop Shop to name a few.

If you love sports, Chicago has many to choose from. If you like football you have the Chicago Bears. If you like basketball you have the Chicago Bulls. If you like hockey you have the Chicago Blackhawks. And, how could you not love America's favorite pastime? For baseball fans, you have the Chicago Cubs and the White Sox. I love Chicago and everything it has to offer. It's an amazing place!

After visiting downtown Chicago many times, I decided I wanted to live there. I made up my mind that I wanted to live in a high-rise condo overlooking the city. I went on the internet and started doing searches for the building I wanted to live in. I found a building right beside the famous John Hancock Building. The building is called Water Tower Place. It's the same building that the one and only Oprah Winfrey lives in. I printed off photos of the building and taped them onto my vision board. I looked at these photos every single day in complete faith and believed that I would live in this building.

I was living in Ohio at the time and wanted to move to Chicago badly. When I set a goal to live in this building, I didn't know anyone in Chicago and I didn't have a penny to my name. However, I simply let my imagination run wild and stared at the photos on my vision board constantly. After days of searching, I finally came across a post on the internet. There was an older woman who had a two bedroom condo on the 22th floor in the building that I wanted to live in. This was it!

Her unit had both a city and lake front view. I saw the photos and immediately fell in love. This is where I was going to live. I not only had photos of the building, but now I had photos of the actual unit I would be living in. This is exactly what I needed for my vision board. I put the photos on my vision board and stared at them for hours every day.

I knew I couldn't afford the rent she was asking for, but I didn't care. I believed I would live there anyway. I called the lady and told her I was moving to Chicago in a couple of weeks on a specific date. I asked her if she would hold the unit for me, but she said she had to rent it right away. She told me if someone else didn't rent it she would call me back. I must admit, I was extremely sad because I figured she would have no problem finding a renter for her place.

Since it didn't look good for me, I went ahead and made other living arrangements. I told a man at another location I would move into his property on the specific date. He said he would hold it for me. His place was an absolute dump in the ghetto. I was extremely depressed even thinking about his place, but I needed to make sure I had a place to live when I arrived in Chicago. In the meantime, I continued to visualize myself living in the high-rise condo on the 22th floor inside Water Tower Place. I wanted to live in that building so badly that I couldn't get it out of my mind. The day finally came when it was time for me to leave Ohio and make my move to Chicago.

The entire drive to Chicago had me feeling depressed. I wanted to live in the wealthy area, not in the drug infested ghetto. I felt helpless.

The closer I got to the ghetto the sicker I became. I was on the verge of throwing up. The neighborhoods I drove through were getting worse and worse the closer I got. There is no way I can live in this area! I was witnessing people doing drug deals on the corner of the street.

As I pulled up to the building that I was about to move into I froze in complete shock. Why didn't I do more research about this location? I can't believe I agreed to this. I was already miserable and I hadn't even walked inside yet. I stood on the sidewalk for a few minutes and prayed that God would somehow get me out of this nightmare. How would he be able to perform a miracle with such short notice? I was absolutely clueless. I was so upset that I almost started crying. My body was completely frozen. I couldn't move.

I opened my trunk and grabbed my bags. As I began walking up the steps to meet the landlord my cell phone started ringing. It came up as an unknown number, but for some reason, I felt in my spirit to answer the call, something I never do.

It was the woman who had the condo on the 22nd floor inside Water Tower Place. She said the person who was supposed to rent her unit from her just backed out and she wanted to give me the chance to move in if I still wanted it. Oh my goodness! Are you kidding me I yelled? She was serious. I asked her if I could come over and move in right now? She said yes! I couldn't believe it! I was jumping for joy on the sidewalk in the middle of the ghetto. I immediately threw my bags back in my car and took off. I never went back to that part of Chicago again. I drove downtown to

Michigan Avenue and moved into the high rise condo that I had visualized for the last few weeks. Talk about the midnight hour! That phone call could not have come at a more perfect time. Do you think that happened by accident? Do you think that was a coincidence? Not even close. That was nothing but faith! That was the power of meditation. That was visualizing my vision board every day for hours and hours. Even though I was about to move into the ghetto, my heart was convinced I would be living in the high-rise condo. I had visualized living in Oprah's building so intensely that it came true. It had to. So, I hope this increases your faith in having a vision board. Keep reading and I'll share some more amazing stories with you.

Chapter Five:

My Brand New Car.

Two weeks after I arrived in Chicago, I drove to Cleveland for a business event. It was in the middle of January and it was freezing outside. As I was driving through the state of Indiana on Interstate 70, my tires went over some black ice. My life was about to change in a split second. My car went air borne and started spinning out of control. I don't know how long my passenger and I were out for, but we woke up to the sounds of loud sirens and the jaws of life cutting my car to pieces. The impact of the crash had us trapped inside the car. Shattered glass was embedded in my skull. It took an entire month for all the glass to leave my body. Cuts and blood was everywhere. It was one of the most tragic moments of my entire life.

My passenger and I would both survive and eventually recover. However, my car was demolished. I didn't have money to get another car, so I either walked, took the train, or rode the bus. In downtown Chicago, owning a car is quite a hindrance unless you're rich. Parking on the street is insanely hard to come by, and if you want to pay for an actual parking spot that will cost you $1,000 per month. So, most people who live in Chicago either walk, take the train, or ride the bus. This worked ok for me while I lived in Chicago.

However, it came time for me to leave Chicago and move south to Orlando, Florida. Living in Orlando was nothing like living in Chicago. I had to have a car to get around in Orlando. I had one tiny problem though. I didn't have any money to buy a new car and my credit sucked.

At this point in my life, I didn't have the prosperous mindset that I have today. So, instead of focusing on a Lamborghini, I only had enough faith for a new Honda Civic. So, I cut out pictures of a brand new, sparkling red, 2008 Honda Civic and put it on my vision board. I walked to the Honda dealership in downtown Chicago and the exact car that I put on my vision board was sitting on the showroom floor. The car was brand new. I accepted it by faith right there on the spot. I opened the car door and sat in the driver's seat. I adjusted the rear view mirror to fit my body. Mentally, I made the car mine.

A car salesman walked up to help me. He told me to follow him back to his desk. When I sat down he asked me if I had good credit for financing? I told him no. He then asked me, how do you think you're going to get a brand new car with bad credit? I told him I didn't know how, but I knew the car belonged to me. I could feel it in my spirit. I told him my God in Heaven would deliver it to me somehow. He rolled his eyes at me.

He had me fill out a credit application anyway, hoping that I might get approved. After he ran my credit he realized I was telling him the truth. He told me there was no way I was going to be able to get that car. I smiled and told him, with God all things are possible! I then left the dealership. I visualized myself sitting in the car, driving the car, and enjoying the car in the Florida sun. When I got back to my place I stared at the car on my vision board for an hour straight. This kind of focusing is a very real process. It's faith in action! Intense faith will manifest things for you in miraculous ways.

I bought a plane ticket from Chicago to Orlando with every penny that I had. I would arrive in Orlando on Friday and start working at my new job on Monday morning. I just knew in my spirit that somehow, some way, I was going to get that brand new Honda Civic. I just didn't know how. That's ok though. I just kept believing and having faith that the car would miraculously be delivered to me in some way. I didn't try to figure out how. I decided I would leave that up to God. On Friday morning, just a few hours before my flight was to leave for Orlando, I received this email from a complete stranger:

Hi Christopher, you don't know me, but I met you a few years ago in Columbus, Ohio at the Arnold Schwarzenegger Bodybuilding Expo. I had you autograph my bodybuilding magazine that you were on the cover of that month. I only talked to you for a few minutes because other people were waiting in line to meet you. However, you were the nicest bodybuilder I had ever met. I just wanted to say it was a pleasure meeting you. If you ever need anything feel free to contact me anytime. Sincerely, Bill.

That was the exact email that I received from Bill. The thing that jumped out of his email the most was, If you ever need anything feel free to contact me anytime. I thought to myself, well I need a car. Bill just told me that if I ever needed anything to contact him. So, I decided to email him back and tell him what had happened. I told him I was in a bad car crash. I told him I just got offered a job as a personal trainer in Florida, but I didn't have a car to get me back and forth once I got there. I asked him if he was a Christian and if he was to please pray for me that God would somehow bring me a car. That's all I said to him in my email.

He emailed me back within one hour and here's what he said: Christopher, I'm so sorry to hear about your car crash. I know you don't know me, but I'm the CEO of a bank. I have perfect credit and plenty of money. You left such a lasting impression on me that I would be honored to buy you a car. Please call me! Sincerely, Bill.

To make a long story short, he told me to go to the Honda dealership once I arrived in Orlando. When I picked out the car that I wanted call him and put him on the phone with the salesman. He said he would take care of the rest. I went to the Honda dealership as soon as I arrived in Orlando. I found the same exact, brand new, sparkling red, 2008 Honda Civic sitting on the showroom floor that I saw in Chicago. I called Bill, put him on the phone with the car salesman, and two hours later, I drove off the car lot with a brand new car without paying a penny for it. It was unbelievable! I drove into an empty parking lot and started to cry. I couldn't believe how miraculously God had come through for me. He used a complete stranger to buy me a brand new car. Do you think that happened by accident? Do you think that was a coincidence? Not even close. That was nothing but faith! I visualized that brand new, sparkling red, 2008 Honda Civic on my vision board so intensely that it came true. It had to. So, I hope this increases your faith in having a vision board. Keep reading and I'll share some more amazing stories with you.

Chapter Six:

Unexpected Money.

A month after I arrived in Florida, I got fired from my job. I was building myself a home-based business on the side of my full time job as a personal trainer and my manager found out. He said that was a conflict of interest and fired me without warning. To have this happen to me after living in Orlando for such a short time was quite a shock. I had only received two paychecks during the month I worked as a personal trainer. So, I needed to come up with some money fast.

The number one question I started asking myself was what am I going to do? Should I look for another job? Should I look for a roommate? Did I even want to stay in Orlando? I had quite a few questions that I needed to answer and I needed to answer them fast. However, I didn't want to think about it. I just wanted to take life easy for once. So, I decided to cut out a picture of a huge stack of hundred dollar bills and put it on my vision board. The picture probably had a million dollars in it. So, I stared at the picture of cash and just trusted that somehow, some way, money would come to me.

I refused to work at a job for someone else in Corporate America ever again, but I needed money fast. I honestly didn't know what to do. I eventually just laid down on my bed and started visualizing money coming to me for an hour every single day. I didn't focus on where the money was going to come from. I just focused on the money coming. I trusted that God was going to bring me money in whatever way he chose.

So, I visualized the stack of hundred dollar bills on my vision board and confessed bible verses about money. As I stared at the stack of cash on my vision board, I confessed the bible verses out loud at the same time. The bible verses that I confessed are:

May the Lord, the God of my ancestors increase me a thousand times and bless me as he has promised. **Deuteronomy 1:11**

The Lord will grant me abundant prosperity. **Deuteronomy 28:11**

God gives me hidden treasures, riches stored in secret places, so that I know that he is The Lord. **Isaiah 45:3**

God gives me wealth and possessions and the ability to enjoy them. This is a gift of God. **Ecclesiastes 5:19**

The blessing of the Lord brings me wealth without painful toil for it.
Proverbs 10:22

I know the grace of my Lord Jesus Christ that he was rich, yet for my sake he became poor, so that I through his poverty will become rich.
2 Corinthians 8:9

I will be enriched in every way so that I can be generous on every occasion.
2 Corinthians 9:11

My God will meet all my needs according to the riches of his glory in Christ Jesus. **Philippians 4:19**

Three months had gone by since I got fired from my job. During this time, I did not pay my rent. After not paying my rent for three months I got an eviction notice on my front door. It said I had forty-eight hours to pay the rent or I must vacate the premises.

Well, my rent was $1,200 a month. So, that meant I had to pay the last three months of rent payments, plus late charges. My total bill due in the next forty-eight hours was $4,200. I didn't have it and I had no idea how to get it. Instead of getting worried and stressed out, I decided to calm myself down and visualize the money on the vision board in complete faith and relaxation. Worrying about a lack of money would only push the money away from me. I needed to get myself to a place of serenity and just trust that all the money I needed would come to me by the deadline.

I laid down on my bed, closed my eyes, and started to see myself having lots of money in my hands. The only thing I saw was hundred dollar bills. I saw all my bills and expenses totally paid in full. I saw myself being completely debt free.

I brought my breathing down to a place of complete tranquility. I was now in a very relaxed state of mind. In my mind, I could now see myself as rich and successful. This was a great feeling to be in. As crazy as this is to believe, here's what happened.

An hour later my cell phone rang. It was my aunt Sharon calling me. I thought that was kind of odd because I hadn't spoken to her in many years. She told me that she had bad news. She said my grandma had just died a couple days ago. Yes, that was bad news for sure. However, I wasn't that sad, simply because I hadn't seen my grandma in at least ten years. She had lived a long and healthy life. My aunt Sharon said she needed my address because my grandparents had left me and my brother in their will. She was going to have the bank send us our inheritance.

This was my mom's parents. My brother and I loved spending time with them when we were growing up. They were a lot of fun. They always took great care of us. As we grew older and moved out of state, we didn't stay in touch with them. Now, many years later, we received this phone call informing us of the bad news. My aunt Sharon said that my brother and I would both be receiving approximately $100,000. I almost fainted. I couldn't believe it.

I had visualized that stack of hundred dollar bills on my vision board so intensely that it came true. It had to. So, I hope this increases your faith in having a vision board. Keep reading and I'll share a couple more amazing stories with you.

Chapter Seven:

My Perfect Soulmate.

In February of 2013, I was living by myself in Wellington, Florida. This is an upscale community right next to West Palm Beach. Wellington is the equestrian capital of the world. I was thirty-four years old and still single. At this point in my life I wanted to find my soulmate and get married.

I was content with being single, but I was lonely quite a bit. I wanted a wife, a best friend, a soulmate. I tried dating sites and those were nothing but a disaster. Women would upload fake photos or they would put up photos of themselves when they were fifty pounds lighter. Dating sites were deceiving. Even the Christian websites were deceiving. Christian Mingle was just as bad at Match.

I prayed to God and asked him to introduce me to my wife. I heard the Holy Spirit ask me what I wanted in a wife? I got out a pen and piece of paper and started writing down exactly what I wanted in my wife. I wrote down everything I could think of. The woman that I was going to marry had to be perfect. Well, perfect for me anyway. I was not going to settle in any way, shape, or form. I also cut out images of what I wanted my wife to look like and put them on my vision board. I started visualizing my perfect soulmate immediately.

The pictures I cut out and the things I wrote down about my perfect soulmate were that she would have blond hair, straight white teeth with a beautiful smile, nice sized breasts, she would eat organic food and workout regularly. She would be a Christian and attend a Holy Spirit filled church. And, as crazy as this sounds, I cut out pictures and wrote down that my perfect soulmate would drink the same beverages that I drink, which are sugar free Monster and Diet Mt. Dew. I told myself that if a woman drank the same beverages that I drink then I knew she had to be my perfect soulmate.

I also cut out pictures that my perfect soulmate would be an entrepreneur and want to live a life of wealth and abundance. She would love traveling the world and she would have a heart for helping people who were less fortunate. I was non-negotiable on these things! If a woman didn't have every single thing that I desired then she wasn't my perfect soulmate. My standards were high and I wasn't ever going to lower them. I made up my mind when I was a child that I was only getting married once in my life.

For me to spend the rest of my life with only one woman, she had to be perfect. No exceptions! I also made a list of things that I refused to accept in my perfect soulmate as well. These things were also non-negotiable.

Some of the things that I wrote down that were absolutely unacceptable in my perfect soulmate were that she couldn't be negative or complain. She would never watch television. She would never go to bars, drink beer, smoke cigarettes, or do any drugs whatsoever, pharmaceutical or recreational. She would never choose anyone else above me. This was only a small fraction of the checklist that she would have to pass in order to be my perfect soulmate. Life is too short to settle down with only one person for the rest of your life if they're not perfect for you. I started visualizing my perfect soulmate immediately.

I took my checklist out and read it every single day. I visualized the pictures on my vision board every single night before I went to sleep. I imagined us kissing, holding hands, working out, traveling the world, laying on the beach, raising our kids, going to church, speaking on stage, and anything else you can imagine. I visualized us doing everything as a couple, as perfect soulmates.

Approximately one week later, I received an email from an old female friend of mine that I grew up with in Ohio. I hadn't talked to her in over fifteen years. She saw that I was living down in Florida and wanted to come visit me. We agreed on a date a few weeks later. She decided to bring her girlfriend Stacy down with her. The two of them stayed with me at my home for a week.

They wanted to take a vacation and get away from their lives in Ohio for a short time. Throughout the week that they stayed with me, I got caught up with my old friend and got to know Stacy a little bit too. Stacy was a full time Registered Nurse at Ohio State University Medical Center, but she wanted to retire from Corporate America and start her own business. She was recently divorced and was a single mother of a little girl. The week flew by and their vacation came to an end. I drove them to the airport, gave them a hug, and said goodbye.

When I arrived back at my house it felt empty. It didn't feel right. It felt like it wasn't even the same house. I thought that it must have been because I just had people with me for a week and now they were gone. However, the emptiness didn't leave. I didn't understand what was wrong.

I couldn't figure out why my house and my heart were so empty. It was driving me crazy. A week after they left my house the Holy Spirit spoke to me in a dream and told me to move to Ohio immediately. I've always been obedient to the voice of the Lord, so I obeyed.

At the time, I taught people how to start their own home-based business for a living. Stacy asked me if I would teach her when she stayed at my house, so I called her and let her know that I was coming to Ohio. She was super excited. I bought a one way plane ticket to Columbus, Ohio. I packed only two bags of clothes and left everything else behind, including my books, clothes, possessions, car, and house. I didn't even think about what I was doing. The date was Friday, August 2nd, 2013. I arrived in Columbus at 11:00 in the morning.

When I picked up my luggage at baggage claim, I started questioning what I had just done. Why did I move to Columbus, Ohio? I hated Ohio! I had an uneasy feeling in my stomach being back in Ohio. I loved southern Florida more than any other place in The United States, and I just left it for Columbus, Ohio. Yuck! I had to remind myself that the Holy Spirit told me to do this and I wasn't going to disobey the voice of God.

I've come to learn to just be obedient when God tells you to do something. Don't ask why, just do it! God knows better than you do and he only has your best interest in mind. Four months after I arrived in Columbus, the Holy Spirit spoke to me again in a dream. In my dream, I was walking down an old dirt road with Jesus. He and I were talking and he said to me: Christopher, the reason why I told you to come to Ohio was so you could meet your perfect soulmate. He said, Stacy is the woman I have chosen for you. I started laughing. I told God that Stacy wasn't even my type. However, something strange happened. For the next twenty-one nights, I had the same exact dream. I started wondering what was going on. This had never happened to me before in my entire life. I prayed to God and asked him; why do I keep having the same dream every night?

He said, I told you Stacy is the woman I have chosen for you. You're going to continue having this dream every single night until you tell her about it. This didn't make sense because Stacy and I weren't even each other's types. We had become great friends, but nothing more than that. I said, there is no way I can tell her about this dream because she'll think I'm crazy. So, God repeated himself and told me again, Stacy is the woman I have chosen for you. You're going to continue having this dream every single night until you tell her about it. So, I worked up the courage and told Stacy, I need to talk to you about something. I met her on Friday night at her apartment. I was sitting on her couch and she finally asked me, what do you want to talk about? I couldn't stall any more. I said, I've really enjoyed getting to know you. I think you're a great person and I love having you as a friend. I love you and your daughter like you're my own family. I would never do anything to ruin our friendship, so please don't let what I'm about to share with you change our relationship in any way. I've been having a really crazy dream for three weeks straight. I prayed to God and asked him why? He told me the reason why he had me come to Ohio was so I could meet my perfect soulmate. He said you're the woman he has chosen for me. He said, you're going to become my wife. Her mouth fell wide open. Are you serious she asked? Yes, I'm very serious. I'm not trying to come onto you Stacy. I love you as a friend, but you're not even my type. No offense! I feel the same way about you Christopher. Ok cool. So, now that I told you about the dream can we just forget about it? Yes, absolutely she said!

Stacy and I worked out together at the gym the next day. Neither one of us can explain what happened, but we immediately felt differently about each other. We were now physically attracted to each other. We started flirting with each other and couldn't understand why. One week later, on November 21st, 2013, at 11:00 in the evening, Stacy asked me to kiss her so she could see how she felt about me. I remember exactly where we were, exactly what we were wearing, and exactly what I said to her after she asked me. I said Stacy, if I kiss you we really will get married because you're going to fall in love with my kisses. She said, prove it!

So, I kissed her and our lips were locked together for an hour straight. We've been inseparable ever since. Just like God told me in my dream, Stacy became my wife. Without telling anyone, Stacy and I went to the courthouse and got married to each other on August 28th, 2014. God changed both of our hearts. The way God brought us together is quite remarkable to say the least. I was living down in Florida and Stacy was living up in Ohio. We were 1,000 miles away from each other. God strategically orchestrated a divine encounter with my wife and my old childhood friend. Stacy bumped into my old female friend in the locker room at the gym one day. They struck up a conversation and then a few weeks later came down to visit me in Florida. As soon as I arrived in Ohio, my old female friend disappeared from both of our lives. You see, I wrote down a thorough description and cut out pictures of what I wanted my perfect soulmate to be like. God brought her to me in his own amazing way. I had visualized my perfect soulmate on my vision board so intensely that she had to come into my life. So, I hope this increases your faith in having a vision board. Keep reading and I'll share one more amazing story with you.

Chapter Eight:

#1 Best Selling Author.

On December 31st, 2016, while most of the world was out drinking beer with their friends, my wife and I were at home setting goals for the upcoming year. My wife and I prayed to God and asked him what he wanted us to do with our lives in the next twelve months. The Holy Spirit wasted no time at all. He very clearly said to me, write a book! Like always, I obeyed. The only thing I thought to write about was what I was good at: helping people lose weight. I was a health and fitness expert for the last twenty years. So, without hesitating, I opened up Microsoft Word and began writing my first book. I titled it:

How To Lose Weight With Intermittent Fasting!

I had never written a book before, so I had no clue what I was doing. I was complete ignorance on fire. I didn't have a manual, a format to follow, or a coach to teach me how to do it. I simply began writing. I was such an expert on nutrition, exercise, and supplementation, that information began rushing out of me. I typed non-stop for twenty-four hours straight. I only left my computer twice to go use the restroom. The rest of the time I was typing away. So, I now had a finished book on my hands, but I had no idea what to do with it. God told me to write a book, but that's all he said. What was I supposed to do now? I didn't know, so I simply asked God. It says this in the Holy Bible:

Ask and it will be given to you; seek and you will find; knock and the door will be opened to you. **Matthew 7:7**

According to that scripture, since I asked God what to do next he was obligated by his word to tell me. The Holy Spirit told me to leave my house and go walk around the mall so I could clear my head. Ok. I didn't understand how that was going to help me with the next step of my book, but I did it any way.

My wife and I went to the mall. After we were there for a while we started walking back to our car. We decided to walk through one side of Barnes and Noble and out the other side to the parking lot where our car was parked. As we walked inside, we noticed a man sitting in the coffee shop that we recognized from our church. We had never spoken to him before, so we figured we should say hello and introduce ourselves. It was January 1st, so he asked us what our goals were for the new year.

I told him that I had just finished writing a book, but I didn't know what to do with it now that it was finished. He kind of smirked, and then said, I'm a published author. I've written sixteen books. I can help you. He then told me the next step to take for my book. Within the next twenty-four hours my book was on Amazon selling to people around the world. It was unbelievable to me how fast everything happened.

Within forty-eight hours of hearing the Holy Spirit tell me to write a book, not only did I write it, but I edited it, published it, and sold my very first copy as well. That is fast! Had I known the book writing process was so simple, I would have written my first book twenty years earlier. Now that my book was selling on Amazon, the Holy Spirit then told me to write my second book.

I decided to title my second book: **Sell Your First Book!** *How To Write, Edit, Publish, & Sell Your Very First Book On Amazon Within 48 Hours From Right Now!*

In this book, I teach people exactly how they too can write, edit, publish, & sell their very first book on Amazon within forty-eight hours just like I did. I give them an exact blueprint to follow that walks them through the book writing process step by step, making it impossible for them to fail.

Once I finished my second book, God told me his plans for me and my wife for 2017. He told us that he wanted us to write books and teach people around the world how to do what we already know: how to lose weight, how to write a book, how to start your own business, how to cure illness, sickness, and disease, and how to use the power of your mind to manifest the life of your dreams. My wife and I obeyed and we've followed through on what he's told us to do. When I wrote my first book neither of us had a clue what we were doing. However, we became extremely passionate about this, so we started investing a lot of time and money into our new business. If we were going to become authors, then we were going to become the best.

As always, we both made new vision boards for the life that we wanted to create. The vision board that I'm holding on the cover of this book is my current vision board. Since this book is about having a vision board, I thought I would put my actual vision board on the cover. I practice what I preach. My current vision board has a picture of Oprah on it because I'm visualizing her interviewing me on her television show. I have a picture of a stack of hundred dollar bills on it because I'm visualizing millions of dollars coming to me this year. I have two pictures of Lamborghini's on it because that's my dream car that I'm visualizing right now in my life. You'll also notice on my vision board that I have written: **New York Times #1 Best-Selling Author**. That's because I'm visualizing myself becoming that.

In the first five months of 2017, I've already written and sold eighteen different books on Amazon to people all over the world. My books have sold to people in ten different countries so far. I've received emails and testimonials from people in China, France, Canada, Australia, India, Germany, Switzerland, Wales, Great Britain, and practically every major city in The United States.

I visualize my books selling thousands and thousands of copies to people every single day all over the world. Five of my eighteen books have already reached the #1 best-seller ranking on Amazon. For someone who has only been a published author for five months to achieve those kinds of results is quite remarkable by anyone's standards. I don't say that to brag or try to impress you, but rather to impress upon you that if I can do it, so can you. I've created several vision boards over the years and I've manifested things off every single one of them. Vision boards work!

If you've never created a vision board before, I highly encourage you to do so immediately. Allow yourself to dream. Allow your imagination to run crazy. You need to put everything you can think of and everything you desire on your vision board. This is your very own vision board, so put whatever you want on it. There won't be another vision board anywhere in the world like it because it's yours. If you dream of owning a Rolls Royce, but know you can't afford it based on the amount of money you earn at your job, you need to put a picture of a Rolls Royce on your vision board. If you dream of owning a ten thousand square foot mansion, but know you can't afford it based on the amount of money you earn at your job, you need to put a picture of a ten thousand square foot mansion on your vision board. It doesn't matter how much money you earn at your job. It doesn't matter if you have bad credit or no credit at all. It doesn't matter if you're homeless right now living in a shack. Nothing in this world matters except what you can dream of. Your job isn't to figure out "how" your goals and dreams are going to manifest. Your only job is to dream big and put pictures of what you dream of on your vision board. As you visualize and meditate on your vision board every day your faith will begin to increase. The more your faith increases the more the light bulb will go off in your head with brilliant idea's. These idea's will tell you what to do, where to go, who to talk to, or just to do nothing at all. Sometimes all you need to do is relax and believe. Millions of people all over the world have manifested miraculous things by visualizing them on their vision boards. You have nothing to lose by creating a vision board, but you could possibly gain everything you've ever dreamed of. Let yourself become a kid again. Start dreaming! Take action right now!

After you read this book would you mind doing me a huge favor please? Would you be kind enough to write me a five star customer review for this book on Amazon? By giving this book a good review it will help me as an author and help this book move up the rankings on Amazon. Your words have power. If you wouldn't mind supporting this book I would be extremely grateful. I would love to hear your feedback. You're welcome to contact me at my personal website anytime. I wish you the very best of success in every area of your life!

Christopher Mitchell
www.ChangeYourLifeOvernight.com

If you enjoyed reading this book, here's more books by the author:

-Sell Your First Book

-Vision Board Success

-Faith Produces Miracles

-My Inspiring True-Life Story

-Money Meditation Manifestation

-Why You're Fat & Sick And How To Fix It

-How To Lose Weight With Intermittent Fasting

-Success! The Secret To Becoming Happy, Healthy, And Wealthy

-How To Make Money As An Author Selling Your Books On Amazon

All books can be purchased from:
www.amazon.com/author/fitchristophermitchell